G000137807

S

S

Eastern Europe

Make the most of your time on Earth

ROUGH GUIDES

25 YEARS 1982–2007

NEW YORK • LONDON • DELHI

Contents

Introduction

EXPERIENCES have always been at the heart of the Rough Guide concept. A group of us began writing the books **25 years ago** (hence this celebratory mini series) and wanted to share the kind of travels we had been doing ourselves. It seems bizarre to recall that in the early 1980s, travel was very much a minority pursuit. Sure, there was a lot of tourism around, and that was reflected in the guidebooks in print, which traipsed around the established sights with scarcely a backward look at the local population and their life. We wanted to change all that: to put a country or a city's popular culture centre stage, to highlight the clubs where you could hear local music, drink with people you hadn't come on holiday with, watch the local football, join in with the festivals. And of course we wanted to push travel a bit further, inspire readers with the confidence and knowledge to break away from established routes, to find pleasure and excitement in remote islands, or desert routes, or mountain treks, or in street culture.

Twenty-five years on, that thinking seems pretty obvious: we all want to experience something real about a destination, and to seek out travel's **ultimate experiences**. Which is exactly where these **25 books** come in. They are not in any sense a new series of guidebooks. We're happy with the series that we already have in print. Instead, the **25s** are a collection of ideas, enthusiasms and inspirations: a selection of the very best things to see or do – and not just before you die, but now. Each selection is gold dust. That's the brief to our writers: there is no room here for the average, no space fillers. Pick any one of our selections and you will enrich your travelling life.

But first of all, take the time to browse. Grab a half dozen of these books and let the ideas percolate … and then begin making your plans.

Mark Ellingham
Founder & Series Editor, Rough Guides

25
Ultimate
experiences
Eastern Europe

Navigating the nocturnal underworld in *Zagreb*

For anyone with more than a passing interest in the far frontiers of amplified music, Zagreb is not so much a city-break as an addiction. Even the habitually staid local tourist office has realized that there is more to life than galleries and opera.

Their monthly *Events and Performances* booklet dutifully details upcoming events in the National Theatre before energetically moving on to page after page of mind-bogglingly varied gigs and club nights in the strangest of places.

Out-of-town gig-hoppers should beware however that Zagreb is an insider's city that requires bat-like navigational instincts.

You could waste an entire evening searching for KSET, a legendary black box of a bar hidden behind grey university buildings. Virtually everyone who is anyone in the experimental-jazz-noise-dub-punk-ska world has played here, usually to a gleeful, packed-to-the-rafters public.

Still more leg-work is required to reach the riverside Močvara ("Swamp"), a former factory building splashed with the sci-fi comic-book murals of deranged artist Igor Hofbauer. Not so much a club as the cultural embassy of a hitherto unmapped country, Močvara offers a seven-days-a-week programme of audacious events.

Spend enough time in Močvara and KSET and you'll probably find out what's going on in an anarcho-punk squat called Villa Kiseljak, whose interior-design amalgam of graffiti art and bits of an old washing machine probably deserves a lifestyle article all to itself.

need to know

For information on what's on, Ⓦ www.zagreb-touristinfo.hr has a pretty good events guide, although you're best advised to go to the sites of individual clubs: a brief surf through Ⓦ www.mochvara.hr, Ⓦ www.kset.org and Ⓦ www.aquarius.hr should set you on your way.

One of the most bizarre fixtures in Zagreb's club calendar is Tuesday nights at *Gjuro II*, when media professionals and arty 20-to-40-somethings frug to a fiendishly effective cocktail of indie and retro sounds. So popular that it's impossible to breathe, never mind get served at the bar, it's the kind of event that would descend into madness, paranoia and violence if it were held in any other European country. In Zagreb, such a squeeze is just another excuse for good-natured flirting. Never will the idea of being crushed to death seem so full of possibilities.

The best Czech pubs are straightforward places: tables, benches, beermats and an endless supply of the best beer in the world. And there are few more atmospheric venues for drinking the stuff in than *Masné kramy*, the complex of medieval butchers' stalls in the southern Bohemian town of České Budějovice (Budweis in German).

Walk into the long central hall, sit down and place a beermat in front of you. Soon enough a waiter will walk round with a large tray of frothing beer mugs and slap one down on your table. As you near the end of the glass, before you've even begun to worry about catching the waiter's eye, you'll have been served another. At which point it becomes clear why the Czechs don't go in for pub crawls. With table service the norm, you need a serious strength of will (and a clear head) to get up and leave. Little surprise then that the Czechs top the world beer consumption league, downing approximately a pint a day for every man, woman and child in the country.

There's another reason why *Masné kramy* is a great place in which to quaff the amber nectar – they serve Budvar, produced by the only major Czech brewery not owned by a multinational. Instead, the brewery still belongs to the Czech state, primarily to stave off a takeover bid by Anheuser-Busch, the world's largest beer producer, responsible for the hugely inferior American Budweiser, or Bud as it's universally known. Litigation over the shared name has been going on for nearly a century, and looks set to continue well into the future. For the moment, however, Budvar is in safe hands and continues to be brewed according to traditional techniques. So enjoy the taste – smooth, hoppy, slightly bitter, with an undercurrent of vanilla – while the going's good.

need to know

České Budějovice is 150km south of Prague (2–3hr by train). *Masné kramy* is just off the old town square on Krajinská. The brewery itself is 2.5km north of the old town; tours take place daily by prior arrangement (☎387 705 111 ◉www.budweiser.cz); 100Kč including a tasting.

For a taste of all the Soviet Union once promised and an illustration of what it has come to, there's nowhere better than the all-Russian Exhibition centre, known by its acronym VDNKh. This enormous park in northeast Moscow is a glorious illustration of Soviet hubris, an exuberant cultural mix 'n' match vision of a world where sixteen republics join hand in socialist hand to present a cornucopia of human achievement, ranging from agricultural tools and farm animals to atomic energy.

Opened in 1939 as the All-Union Agricultural Exhibition, the grounds were extended in the 1950s to include culture, science and technology, and continued to expand till 1989. Nevertheless, the overall atmosphere is of prewar optimism, when all progress was good and man was master of the world, living in a kind of mechanized agricultural paradise where even the streetlights were shaped like ears of corn.

Set around the gaudy gold fountain of the Friendship of Nations, pavilions for the former Soviet socialist republics and areas of economic achievement make a gesture towards national building styles while remaining unmistakably Stalinist. Particularly striking are the Ukraine Pavilion, a sparkling mosaic and majolica jewelbox; the Uzbekistan Pavilion, patterned with interlocking geometric designs; and the stylish, Art-Deco-influenced Grain Pavilion. Beyond, a copy of the rocket which took Yuri Gagarin into space points skywards in front of the Aerospace pavilion. Built in 1966, the pavilion's railway-station-like hangar and glass dome are still breathtaking in their vastness.

It's a little disappointing to find the working models of hydroelectric power stations and the herds of prize cattle long gone, and even the famous Soviet worker and collective farm girl monument vanished recently amid rumours that it's been melted down for scrap metal. But the casual traders and cheap beer stands that now fill VDNKh lend the place a certain raffish charm. Perhaps it's fitting that the monumental worker and farm girl have been replaced by a succinct image of today's Russia: rows of salesmen from the Caucasus selling everything from Belarusian bras to cheap Chinese trainers under the Aerospace Pavilion's thousand unlit light bulbs.

need to know

The exhibition grounds are located near metro station VDNKh. For a virtual excursion of the park in English see ⓦ www.vvcentre.ru/eng/about_us/excursion/

Soviet **3**
Exhibitionism
in **Moscow**

Beavering in the Lahemaa National Park, Estonia

Visitors to Lahemaa National Park, a 725-square-kilometre area of pastureland and wilderness that runs along Estonia's northern seaboard, are often frustrated by never setting eyes on the forest-roaming bears, moose and lynx that guidebooks promise. The best they can hope for is the fleeting glimpse of a deer or rabbit – hardly the thing of which travellers' tales are made. Beavers, however, are a different matter. Although they're just as elusive as many of their peers (you'd probably need infra-red vision and the patience of an Easter Island statue to actually see one in action), evidence of their activity is everywhere. My own induction into beaver-world occurred at the Oandu beaver trail, a well-marked nature walk that begins on the eastern fringes of the park. Embracing dense forest, desolate bogs, coastal wetlands and archaic fishing villages, Lahemaa is the best possible introduction to this Baltic country's unspoiled rural character.

Leading through thick woodland, the trail crosses several streams where log-built dams and freshly gnawed tree-trunks indicate the presence of a highly industrious animal. Beavers are the architects of the animal world, endlessly redesigning their environment until it meets their bark- and twig-munching requirements. The main missions of a beaver's life is to carve out a feeding area by felling trees, building a dam, and flooding an area of forest that other herbivores are loath to enter. Free of competition, it can then merrily stuff its face with all the vegetal matter trapped within its semi-sunken realm.

These beaver-created landscapes can be found throughout the Baltic States. The Pedvale open-air sculpture park in Latvia even includes a "Mr Beaver" in its list of featured artists – a real-life furry prankster who mischievously flooded part of the grounds.

Despite two years of trawling through the protected areas of the Baltics, the only beaver I set eyes on was the tombstone-toothed cartoon character who appeared nightly to advertize toothpaste on Lithuanian television. When I finally came face to face with one, it was basking in Mediterranean sunshine in the middle of a Croatian zoo. It would be nice to think that, somewhere in a dank Baltic forest, there's a birch tree with his name on it.

need to know

The Lahemaa National Park lies an hour's drive east of the Estonian capital Tallinn. The National Park visitors' centre (☎ 0372 329 5555, Ⓦ www.lahemaa.ee) is in in Palmse.

"At the moment of the birth of our planet, the most beautiful meeting of land and sea was on the Montenegrin coast", gushed Lord Byron back in the nineteenth century. Since then, much has happened to this tiny and outrageously beautiful country, most importantly in 2006 when it became the last of the ex-Yugoslav republics to gain independence. Sprinkled along its short-but-sweet 300-kilometre-long coastline is a multiplicity of comely fishing villages, ancient stone walled towns and energetic beach resorts.

Should you be thirsting for a drop of culture, make a beeline for breathtaking Kotor, a UNESCO-protected, medieval-walled town huddled under the gaze of Mount Lovčen, Montenegro's holiest mountain, and framed by a series of spectacular inland fjords. For more razzle-dazzle, head to the lively resort of Budva, a short drive or ferry trip south. Its long, curving pebble beach is packed with young sun-worshippers, while the many vine-covered restaurants stretched along the esplanade do a roaring trade serving up enormous plates of *kačamak* (white flour, potato and melted *kajmak*, a creamy cheese) and *raštan* (dried smoked ribs with cabbage). Later on, as the sun dips, bars and cafés dispense glasses of Vranac, the local red wine, and Loza, a fiery, throat-tingling grape brandy.

Sveti Stefan is the coast's most iconic site. Linked to the mainland by a taper thin concrete causeway, this magnificent walled island – complete with luxurious hotel – was once a popular retreat for Tito, who also entertained superstar celebrities such as Elizabeth Taylor and Richard Burton here. With its laid-back charm and lack of pretence, the Montenegrin coast is a cracking place to be right now, before the crowds return.

need to know

Any of the coastal resorts can be easily accessed by bus from Podgorica, the Montenegrin capital (which is also served by a daily train from Belgrade), or from Dubrovnik, just across the border in Croatia.

5 Chilling out on the Montenegrin coast

Bathing matters in Budapest, it really does. Indeed, few activities are as important to Budapesters as a daily dip in one of the city's splendid **Art Nouveau** thermal baths (*gyógyfürdő*). From the magnificently appointed Gellért baths complete with gorgeous majolica tiles and mosaics, to the palace-like majesty of Széchenyi and its enormous mixed-sex outdoor pool, Budapest's love affair with bathing has been around a long time; since **Roman times**, in fact, when the first springs were discovered north of the city.

So, **what do you do** once there? The bathing ritual can be confusing, even daunting for non-native speakers, especially because little information is written in English and few attendants speak anything other than Hungarian and German. Having bought your ticket, which usually entitles you to a two-hour stint in the sauna, steam room and pools (you can pay extra for a massage or a mud bath), head to the changing room. Here the attendant will direct you to a cabin, whereupon you will be given a **kötény** – a sliver of a loincloth for a man or an apron for a woman – which just about covers the essentials. Indeed, in many of the single-sex steam baths, swimsuits are still rare so if you're the bashful type, this is the perfect opportunity for you to **lose those inhibitions**. Once changed, lock up and in you go. The done thing is to take a sauna, have a dip in the warm pool, a relaxing stint in the steam room, an icy cold plunge (brrr!), followed by a delicious, **spine-tingling** hot plunge – and then repeat this marvellous ritual all over again. Whether here to soak as is common in many pools, to participate in games of chess, men and women of all ages, shapes and sizes happily can be found bobbing up and down. As the **quintessential Hungarian experience**, taking to the waters really does take some beating.

need to know

Both the Széchenyi (Állatkerti körút 11) and Gellért (Kelenhegyi út 4) baths are open daily 6am–7pm (€10). Tickets cover entrance and locker; towels, bathrobes and bathing caps are rented separately. Bring your own chess set.

6 Taking to the waters in Budapest, Hungary

Few figures capture the imagination as dramatically as Dracula, the bloodthirsty vampire count from deepest darkest Transylvania – at least that's how Bram Stoker portrayed the mythical version in his 1897 novel. The real Dracula was in fact the fifteenth-century Wallachian prince Vlad Țepeș, better known as Vlad the Impaler. Although never accused of vampirism, his methods of execution – spread-eagled victims were bound and a stake hammered up their rectum, then raised aloft and left to die in agony – earned him a certain notoriety, especially amongst his long-time adversaries, the anti-crusading Turks, who pathologically feared him.

Inevitably, the legend of Dracula is touted for all it's worth, but finding anything meaningful associated with Vlad is tricky. Aside from his birthplace in the delightful town of Sighișoara – now a high-class if kitschy restaurant – the most played-up Dracula connection is in the small southern Transylvanian town of Bran. Looking every inch like a vampire count's residence, the splendidly sited Bran Castle is hyped as Dracula's haunt and encompassed by an army of souvenir stalls flogging vampire tack. The more mundane reality, however, is that Vlad may have laid siege to it once.

Dracula's real castle lies in the foothills of the stunning Făgăraș mountains in northern Wallachia. Located just north of the village of Arefu, a steep hillside path – an exacting climb up 1400 steps – brings you to Poienari Castle, one of Vlad's key fortresses and where, allegedly, his wife flung herself out of a window, exclaiming that she "would rather have her body rot and be eaten by the fish of the Argeș" than be captured by the Turks. Aside from some reasonably intact towers, this surprisingly small citadel is now little more than a jumble of ruins. However, its dramatic setting ensures an authentically spooky atmosphere, no doubt the sort that Bram Stoker had in mind when penning his masterpiece about the ultimate horror icon.

need to know

Hourly buses go from Brașov to Bran Castle (Tues–Sun 9am–6pm; €3). For Poienari (daily 9am–5pm; free) take a bus (7 daily) from Curtea de Argeș to Arefu, from where it's 4km to the footpath that leads up to the castle. *Casa Dracula*, the restaurant occupying Dracula's birthplace, is at Str Cositorarilor 5 (daily 10am–midnight).

7

Countless castles:
on the Dracula
trail in Romania

08

ST PETERSBURG'S
WILD WHITE NIGHTS

Imagine spending all day sightseeing, taking a shower and a nap, and then looking out of the window to see the sky as bright as midday. Your body kicks into overdrive, and the whole day seems to lie ahead of you. The streets throng with people toting guitars and bottles of champagne or vodka; naval cadets and their girlfriends walking arm in arm, and pensioners performing impromptu teadances on the riverbank. The smell of black tobacco mingles with the perfume of lilac in parks full of sunbathers. It's eight o'clock in the evening, and St Petersburg is gearing up for another of its wild White Nights.

Freezing cold and dark three months of the year, St Petersburg enjoys six weeks of sweltering heat when the sun barely dips below the horizon – its famous White Nights or *Byele Nochy*. Children are banished to dachas in the countryside with grandparents, leaving parents free to enjoy themselves. Life becomes a sequence of *tsusovki* (gatherings), as people encounter long-lost friends strolling on Nevsky prospekt or feasting in the Summer Garden at midnight.

To avoid disrupting the daytime flow of traffic, the city's bridges are raised from 2am onwards to allow a stream of ships to sail upriver into Russia's vast interior. Although normally not a spectacle, during White Nights everyone converges on the River Neva embankments to watch, while bottles are passed from person to person, and strangers join impromptu sing-songs around anyone with a guitar or harmonium – chorusing folk ballads or "thieves' songs" from the Gulag. Those with money often hire a boat to cruise the canals that wend through the heart of the city.

The bridges are briefly lowered during the middle of the night, allowing queues of traffic fifteen minutes to race across. Keeping in lane is entirely ignored, with drivers jockeying for position as if it was a chariot race. By this time, people are stripping off and jumping into the Neva – those too prodigiously drunk to realize go swimming fully clothed.

> **need to know**
> The White Nights officially lasts from June 11 to July 2, but nights are short and celebratory for two weeks on either side. Reserve your accommodation at least a month in advance.

23

Balkan brass madness,
Guča, Serbia 9

Bars, restaurants and tents blast out hard Romani funk, punters slap Serbian dinar notes on to the heads of sweat-soaked musicians, and men and women of all ages and dispositions form a *kolo* – a joyous, fast-paced circular formation dance. For one week each summer, the otherwise tranquil village of Guča (pronounced goo-chah), located some 250km south of the Serbian capital Belgrade, is transformed into the undisputed party capital of the Balkans. Guča is home to the Dragačevo Trumpet Festival, the largest, loudest – and quite possibly, craziest – event of its kind anywhere in the world. Essentially a celebration of folk and brass music from across the Balkans, principally Serbia, it stars dozens of bands competing for the coveted Golden Trumpet.

The king of Guča, and the finest trumpet player of his generation, is Boban Markovič who, with his fabulous twelve-piece orchestra – which includes his teenage son Marko – has scooped the Golden Trumpet several times. Such has been their dominance that they

no longer bother competing for the big prize, though they do still make the occasional feted appearance. Markovič is typical of the large number of Roma, or Gypsy, musicians that attend Guča, and who make this event the rocking spectacle that it is. With their ecstatic, turbo-charged sounds, these outrageously talented and charismatic performers provide a potent sonic odyssey – indeed, in what is an oft-repeated quote, Miles Davis was once moved to remark "I never knew a trumpet could be played like that". Welcome to Guča, welcome to brass madness.

need to know

The Guča festival takes place over four or five days in August with cultural events as well as concerts taking place from morning till night. Buses (€20 return) depart from Belgrade. See ⓦwww.guca. co.yu for more information and music downloads.

I'd never seen an Art Nouveau power station until I went to Łódź. I found it while strolling through the south-central district of Księży Młyn, an enormous complex of red-brick mill buildings and workers' tenements built by Karl Scheibler, a nineteenth-century textile magnate of megalomaniacal ambition. Seduced by the seemingly derelict building's sensuously curvy facade I advanced through a half-open door to be greeted by an enthusiastic group of trainee rock-climbers dangling on ropes from the wall of the main turbine hall. Below them, antiquated generators and instrument panels stood on parade like exhibits in an art gallery. It was a suitably bizarre introduction to the most unexpectedly absorbing of Polish cities.

If Florence is a must-visit for anyone keen to get to grips with the Renaissance, then Łódź should be an essential stop-off for those interested in the Industrial Revolution. Once dubbed the "Polish Manchester" on account of its thriving textile industry, the city still throngs with soaring chimneys and fortress-like mill buildings of extraordinary, temple-like beauty. Many of the mills went bankrupt after the collapse of communism in 1989, and economically-depressed Łódź became as unfashionable as it is unpronounceable ("Woodge", by the way, is how you actually say it).

Like the original Manchester, however, Łódź* is in the throes of reinventing itself as a mecca for modish lifestyles rather than manufacturing might. Central to the city's rebranding is the Manufaktura, a revitalization project of gargantuan proportions which has taken a post-industrial graveyard of abandoned warehouses on the fringes of the centre, and stuffed it with shopping malls, cinemas and coffee bars. Running along the southern flanks of the Manufaktura complex is the erstwhile Poznański Factory, whose castellated façade stands in eloquent testimony to the self-aggrandizing tastes of nineteenth century Łódź's mercantile elite. Textile pharaoh Izrael Poznański lived next door to his factory in the Poznański Palace (now the town museum), whose rooms are opulently decorated with flamboyant woodcarving, stuccoed nymphs and stained glass. Rumour has it that Poznański didn't quite understand what his architect meant by terms such as Neo-classical, Neo-renaissance and Neo-baroque, and so enthusiastically ordered all three. With a shopping list such as this, Łódź's new mall-cruising culture couldn't have wished for a more appropriate forefather.

need to know

The Municipal Museum, inside the Poznański palace at ul. Ogrodowa 15 (Tues & Thurs 10am–4pm, Wed 2–6pm, Fri–Sun 10am–2pm), provides an overview of the city's industrial heritage.

Mills and malls: on the industrial heritage trail in Łódź

Jewish 11 Vilnius

For a city that suffered countless occupations in the twentieth century, and has been renamed at least three times, Vilnius – Wilno (Polish) or Vilna (Russian) as was – is a surprisingly self-confident place. Compact and attractive, it has an active café scene and a vibrant not-too-boisterous nightlife. On its streets of well-dressed inhabitants chatting amiably on mobile phones and head-scarved old women selling icons, it's possible to find vestiges of its previous incarnations, from Polish statues to Russian Orthodox churches. But with the destruction wrought during World War II and subsequent Soviet control over the city's reconstruction, it is its unofficial name, "the Jerusalem of the North" – allegedly donned by Napoleon – that leaves you wondering what is left today of one of Europe's most significant Jewish communities, devastated by the Nazis.

need to know
The Jewish State
Museum is at
Pylimo 4 and
Paménkalnio 12.
Paneriai lies 10km
southwest of the
city centre.

Vilnius'
Jewish quarter centres around
the aptly named Žydu gatve – "Jews'
Street". As interest is rekindled in the city's Jewish
past, old Yiddish shop signs are being uncovered
and restored and it's possible, through photos at the
Jewish museum, to see what a vigorous mass of kosher
butchers, matzoh makers and tailors vying for business this
once was. From a prewar tally of more than a hundred synagogues,
Vilnius now has only one, but many religious items were saved from
destruction, including Torah scrolls and menorah, and are now displayed at the
museum. The lively secular life of the Jewish population is well represented too, with a
fascinating collection of Yiddish theatre posters and sports club memorabilia.

In contrast, the showcases at the museum in Paneriai, the forest where most of Vilnius's
Jews were killed, hold only a few stark items taken from the pits in which people were shot:
rusty keys, an engraved comb, a pair of spectacles, a child's ragged toy – these few personal
belongings representing the thousands who were murdered here.

Lithuania lost nearly 95 percent of its Jewish population in the Holocaust. At an exhibition
about people who risked their lives to hide Jews during the war, I stop in front of a photograph
of a couple with a baby. A woman approaches. "That's me" she smiles, pointing at the baby. "I
was born in hiding." A group of Lithuanian schoolchildren stare in fascination and immediately
crowd around her; she patiently answers their eager questions.

You have to see the task of finding the all-important kľúč (key) as part of the experience when visiting the wooden churches of Slovakia's Carpathian foothills. Sure enough, there's nearly always a little sign (in Slovak) pinned to the wooden door, telling you which house harbours it, but finding the right one in a village without street names and only (often fairly random) house numbers, is a feat in itself. It's a sure way to get to meet the local head-scarved babičky (grannies), but don't expect to get to see too many churches in one day.

The churches look like something straight out of an East European fairy tale, or a Chagall painting: perched on slight hillocks by the edge of the woods, looking down on their villages, their dark brown shingled exterior sprouting a trio of onion domes. Most were built in the eighteenth century when the influence of Baroque was making itself felt even among the carpenter architects of the Carpathians. Once inside, you can't help but be struck by the musty murkiness of the dark wooden interiors. At one end a vast and vibrantly decorated iconostasis reaches from the floor to the ceiling, its niches filled with saints. Elsewhere, a local folk artist allows his imagination to go wild in a gory depiction of the Last Judgement, with the damned being burned, boiled and decapitated with macabre abandon.

Despite the fact that the churches are more often than not locked, they're still very much in use, mostly (but not exclusively) by the Greek Catholic church, a unique strand of Roman Catholicism. Should you happen upon one when there's a service, note that mass is celebrated in Old Slavonic.

need to know

The churches are scattered across a remote part of Slovakia – by far the easiest way to reach them is to hire a car or a bicycle. However, those listed below are all a day's hike from either Bardejov or Svidník, the two main towns of the region, both of which have train stations: Dobroslava lies 7km north of Svidník, Hervatov 8km southeast of Bardejov, Ladomírová 4km northeast of Svidník and Miroľa, 12km east of Svidník.

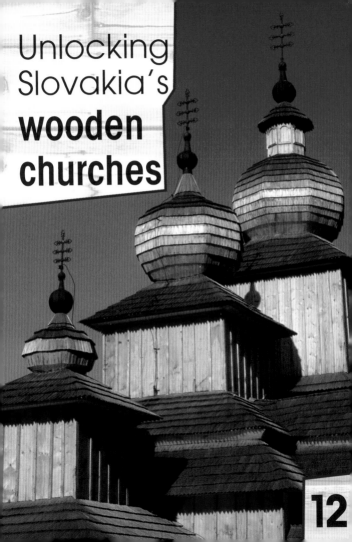

Unlocking Slovakia's
wooden churches

12

It is the quintessential Balkan city, a noisy, vigorous metropolis, whose nightlife is as varied as it is exciting, and whose sophisticated citizens really know how to party hard. For these reasons, Belgrade has every right to proclaim itself the good-time capital of Eastern Europe. As good a place as any to start is Strahinjiča bana, otherwise known as Silicone Valley owing to the number of surgically enhanced women who parade up and down here. You can get the evening going with a glass of hoppy Nikšičko beer or shot of šljivovica (a ferocious plum brandy) in one of the many über-hip bars packed cheek-by-jowl along this fantastically lively street. From here it's time to hit Andergraund, a venerable techno joint located in the vast catacombs beneath the Kalemegdan citadel. Complete with a funky chill-out zone, this vibrant and popular place is typical of the city's clubs, and though the scene is in a constant state of flux, good dance venues are the rule rather than the exception.

To experience a different side to Belgrade's nightlife, head down to the banks of the Danube and Sava rivers which, during the summer months, are lined with a multitude of river rafts (splavovi), variously housing restaurants, bars and discos, or a combination of all three. These places can get seriously boisterous, but are popular with devotees of Serbia's infamous turbo-folk music, a brilliantly kitsch hybrid of traditional folk and

Having a blast in Belgrade, Serbia

electronic pop. If this type of music presses your buttons – and it is worth experiencing at least once – you can also check out one of the city's several Folkotekes, discos specializing in turbo-folk. Another quirky, yet somewhat more restrained, Belgrade institution is the hobby bar; these are small, privately owned cafés or bars, run by young entrepreneurs ostensibly for the entertainment of their pals, though anyone is welcome to visit. The next morning the chances are that you'll be good for nothing more than a cup of strong Turkish coffee in one of the many cafés sprawled across Trg Republike – before doing it all over again that same evening.

need to know

Anderground is at Pariski 1a (daily 10am–4am). A good hobby bar is Lokal u Pripremi, at Skadarska 40a (daily 1pm–4am). Strahinjiča bana, Obilićev venac and Njegoševa ulica, offer the greatest concentration of bars and cafés.

13

14 *Following* the way of the
Goat in highland
Bulgaria

need to know
In Kovachevitsa, Kapsuzovi kushti (☎ 899 403 089,
ⓦ Ekapsazovs_houses@yahoo.com) offers fully-
equipped rooms and a fantastic restaurant. Alternatively
contact Sofia-based Zig-Zag Holidays (☎ 980 3200,
ⓦ www.zigzagbg.com), who can book accommodation
throughout Bulgaria.

Most people tend to use an alarm clock, but in rural Bulgaria you can rely on goats to get you out of bed. In the east Bulgarian village of *Zheravna*, an age-old Balkan ritual is enacted daily between 6 and 7am, when the local goatherd takes the beasts to pasture, collecting them one by one from the individual households where they spend the night. Bells clanging raucously as they pass, it makes for a novel dawn chorus.

With tumbledown stone houses leaning over crooked cobbled alleyways, *Zheravna* is a perfect example of a village whose rustic character has remained largely unchanged since the nineteenth century. Goat farming is no longer the most lucrative of industries, however, and rural depopulation has all but emptied the place of its young. Nowadays, the renovation of old houses and the development of rustic B&Bs points at a tourist-friendly future.

Zheravna is far from being the only remote community whose combination of highland scenery, historic architecture and hospitable landladies has made it a crucial stop-off on any village-hopping itinerary. Lying at the end of a potholed mountain road in Bulgaria's rugged southwest, *Kovachevitsa* is a bewitching knot of half-timbered houses and full of no-frills accommodation: just don't expect to see "vacancy" signs hanging outside gateways or tourist offices taking reservations. Instead, *Kovachevitsa*'s mayoress hangs around at the village tavern keeping an eye open for any approaching cars bearing registration plates she doesn't immediately recognize. She then, goat-herding instincts intact, guides the newcomers to the house of a granny she knows who has a double bed made up and ready. Breakfast will include locally-made herbal teas, and yoghurt so healthy it could add years to your life.

There's not a great deal to do when you get here, although that is undoubtedly part of the attraction. Lolling around in wildflower-carpeted meadows and meditating in the middle of a pine forest are just two of the activities on offer. If stuck for ideas you could always follow the goats, whose taste for invigorating air and gourmet grasses will lead you up into some of the most exhilarating wilderness areas in Europe.

15
Stalagmites, stalactites and a human fish in
Slovenia

Of Slovenia's many show caves, none has quite the pulling power of Postojna, located in the heart of the country's beguiling Karst region. And, at more than 20km long, it is Europe's most expansive cave system. Writing about Postojna in the seventeenth century, the great Slovene polymath Janez Vajkard Valvasor remarked: "in some places you see terrifying heights, elsewhere everything is in columns so strangely shaped as to seem like some creepy-crawly, snake or other animal in front of one", an apt description for this immense grotto – a jungle of impossibly shaped stalactites and stalagmites, gothic columns, and translucent stone draperies, all of which are the result of millions of years of erosion and corrosion of the permeable limestone surface by rainwater. Postojna has been Slovenia's most emblematic tourist draw ever since Emperor Franz Josef I set foot here in 1819, though the smudged signatures etched into the craggy walls would indicate an earlier human presence in the caves, possibly as far back as the thirteenth century. Visiting the cave first entails a two-kilometre-long ride through narrow tunnels on the open-topped cave train – a somewhat more sophisticated version compared to the hand-pushed wagons used in the nineteenth century – before you emerge into the vast chambers of formations and colours. Among them there's the Beautiful Cave, which takes its name from the many lustrous features on display; the Spaghetti Hall, so-called because of its thousands of dripping, needle-like formations; and the Winter Chamber, which is home to a beast of a stalagmite called "Brilliant", on account of its dazzling snow-white colour.

Despite all this, Postojna's most prized asset, and most famous resident, is *proteus anguinus*, aka the Human Fish. This enigmatic 25-

centimetre-long, pigmentless amphibian has a peculiar snake-like appearance, with two tiny pairs of legs – hence the name – and a flat, pointed fin to propel itself through water. Almost totally blind, and with a lifespan approaching one hundred years, it can also go years without food, though it's been known to dabble in a spot of cannibalism. Indeed, the abiding memory for many visitors to Postojna is of this most bizarre and reclusive of creatures slinking about its dimly lit tank.

need to know
The caves are located 2km north of Postojna town centre; there is no public transport but it's an easy walk. Tours, lasting ninety minutes, take place daily on the hour from 9am until 6pm (€15).

The Hermitage's collections run the gamut of the ancient world and European art. Where else could you find Rubens, Matisse, prehistoric dope-smoking gear and the world's largest vase under one roof?

The museum occupies the Imperial Winter Palace and the Old and New Hermitages, added by successive Tsars. To avoid the crowds, start by checking out the little-visited ancient Siberian artefacts in the palace's dingy ground-floor west wing. The permafrost preserved burial mounds that contained mum nd chariots – all discovered by Soviet archeologists 2500 years later. They even found a brazier encrusted with marijuana – Altai nomads used to inhale it inside miniature tents –which was still potent.

Next, luxuriate in the State Rooms, glittering with gold leaf and semi-precious stones. The Malachite Drawing Room has an underwater feel, being awash with the eponymous green stone. The Provisional Government met there until their arrest by the Bolsheviks. On certain days, the English Peacock Clock spreads its bejewelled tail in the Pavilion Hall, whose decor fuses Islamic, Roman and Renaissance motifs. By this time the tour groups are thinking of lunch, making it a good time to investigate the art collection.

The adjacent Old and New Hermitage are stuffed with antiquities and artworks and it's difficult knowing where to turn. Old Masters are on the first floor – Botticelli, Van Dyck and twenty paintings by Rembrandt (including *Danaë*, restored after a deranged visitor slashed it) – plus works by Velázquez and Goya. If you prefer more modern art, be overwhelmed by Renoirs, Van Goghs, and Gauguins – all "trophy art" taken from Nazi Germany in 1945. The Post-Impressionist collection on the top floor has a superb array of Matisses and Picassos, acquired by two Muscovite philanthropists in the 1900s. Matisse's *Music* and *Dance* were commissioned for his patron's mansion, whose owner feared that the nude flautist might offend guests, and painted out his genitals – which the Hermitage's restorers have carefully restored.

Merely glancing at each item in the collection would take nine years to see the whole lot. With not quite so much time on your hands, you may prefer to browse what you missed in one of the many catalogues, from the comfort of a nearby café.

need to know

The Hermitage is on Palace Square, near Nevsky Prospekt metro. Ordering a ticket online ($17.95; ⓦ www.hermitage.org) gives you a voucher allowing

16

A MINDBLOWING MUSEUM - ST PETERSBURG'S HERMITAGE

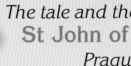
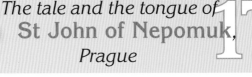
As you shuffle along with your fellow tourists round the chancel of Prague's main cathedral, there's not a lot to see beyond the remains of a few medieval Czech kings with unpronounceable names – Břetislav, Spytihněv, Bořivoj. That is, until you find your way virtually barred by a giant silver tomb, which looks for all the world as if it has been abandoned by a bunch of Baroque builders upon discovering it was too big to fit into one of the side chapels. Turning your attention to the tomb itself, you're faced with one of the most gobsmackingly kitsch mausoleums imaginable. Sculpted in solid silver, with air-borne angels holding up the heavy drapery of the baldachin, you notice the saint's rather fetching five-star sunburst halo, and back-to-back with him, a cherub proudly pointing to a glass case. On closer inspection, you realize the case contains a severed tongue.

Jesuits were nothing if not theatrical, and here, in the tomb of their favourite martyr, St John of Nepomuk, the severed tongue adds that extra bit of macabre intrigue. Arrested, tortured and then thrown – bound and gagged – off the Charles Bridge, John was martyred in 1393 for refusing to divulge the secrets of the queen's confession to the king. A cluster of stars appeared above the spot where he was drowned – or so the story goes – and are depicted on all his statues, including the one on the Charles Bridge. The gruesome twist was added when the Jesuits had his corpse exhumed in 1715 and produced what they claimed was the martyr's tongue – alive and licking so to speak – and stuck it in the glass case. Unfortunately, science had the last say, and in 1973 tests proved that the tongue was in fact part of his decomposed brain. Sadly, the object you now see on his tomb is a tongue-shaped replica.

need to know

St Vitus Cathedral in Prague Castle is open daily. To visit the tomb, you must buy a ticket (220–350Kč depending on how much more of the castle you wish to visit). Charles Bridge can be visited any time of the day or night. For more on John, see ⓦ www.sjn.cz.

TACKLING
Old Mr Three Heads
Slovenia

It's said that every Slovene has to climb Mount Triglav, the country's highest (2864m) and most exalted peak at least once in their lifetime. They're joined by hikers and climbers from many nations, who arrive in droves each summer. The mountain's nickname, Old Mr Three Heads (Triglav means "Three Heads"), originated with the early Slavs, who believed that it accommodated a three-headed deity who watched over the earth, sky and underworld.

The most difficult approach is via the indomitable north face, a stark 1200-metre-high rock wall, certainly not for the faint-hearted. Most hikers opt for the route from Lake Bohinj further south – watched over by steeply pitched mountain faces, this brooding body of water is the perfect place to relax before embarking on the mountain trail ahead.

Not only is Triglav a tough nut to crack in one day, but these convivial refuges are great places to catch up with fellow hikers as well as refuel with a steaming goulash and a mug of sweet lemon-infused tea. Most people push on at the crack of dawn, eager to tackle the toughest part of the ascent, entailing tricky scrambles, before the triple-crested peak of Triglav looms into view. Once completed, according to tradition, there's just one final act for first-timers, namely to be "birched" – in other words, soundly thrashed across the buttocks with a birch branch.

Starting at the lake's western shore, you pass the spectacular Savica Waterfall, before a stiff climb over the formidable Komarča cliff, and then a more welcome ramble through meadows and pastureland. Beyond here lies the highlight of this route: rich in alpine and karstic flora, the Valley of the Seven Lakes is a series of beautiful tarns surrounded by majestic limestone cliffs. The views are glorious, though by this stage most hikers are hankering after the simple comforts of a mountain hut.

need to know
Agencies in Bohinj offer two-day organized treks of Triglav from €150. The best time for climbing is May, June or September, but always take suitable clothing and sufficient provisions. For a map, try the 1:50,000 Triglav National Park by the Alpine Association of Slovenia.

19 Hungary's golden mouldie: drinking Tokaj in ancient wine cellars

Eastern European wine receives few accolades. Apart from one, that is: the "wine of kings, the king of wines", was how Louis XVI described Tokaj, Hungary's most celebrated drink – indeed, so important is it to Hungarians that it's even cited in the national anthem.

Harvested amongst the rolling green hills of the Tokaj-Hegyalja region in northeast Hungary, the most famous variety of Tokaj is Aszú, a devilishly sweet dessert wine that owes its distinctive character to the region's volcanic loess soil and the prolonged sunlight that prevails here. More importantly, though, it's down to the wine-making techniques employed, whereby the grapes are left to become overripe, leading to botrytization – in layman's terms, attacked by rot (grandly termed the "noble rot" in these parts). This shrivels the grapes to raisin-sized proportions and gives them their concentrated sweetness.

The best time to sample the wine is during the Grapes Harvest Festival, which takes place each October in, appropriately enough, the pretty town of Tokaj. Celebrating the wine's maturation, this merry jamboree features live folk music and open-air dancing, goulash cooking competitions and, best of all, a "wine-ship", which entails much consumption of the season's vintage whilst cruising the Tisza river.

Otherwise, nothing beats a few hours in one of the cosy cellars lining the town's narrow streets, the most venerable of which is the Rákóczi cellar, named after the seventeenth-century prince, Ferenc Rákóczi. Reposed in 24 eerily cobwebbed, chandelier-lit passages are thousands upon thousands of bottles of the region's choicest wines. No less esteemed is the cellar of the same name located in the town of Sárospatak; it was here that Rákóczi would come to smoke his pipe, indulge in his favourite tipple, and plot the downfall of the Habsburgs. Hewn out by prisoners from the castle dungeons, the kilometre-long cellar, chock-full of handsome oak barrels, is thickly coated with penész, the "noble mould" – everything's noble where Tokaj is concerned – whose presence is integral to the wine's flavour. Whether quaffing this most regal of wines in the open air, down a cellar, or on a boat, the taste of Tokaj is something you won't forget in a hurry.

need to know

The Rákóczi cellar in Tokaj is at Kossuth tér 15 (mid-March to mid-Oct daily 10am–6pm); the cellar in Sá'rospatak is at Erzsébet utca tér 26 (same times); a tasting of six wines plus nibbles costs around €8.

EccENtrIC ARCHITECTURE:
wandering the streets of Rīga

Walking along Alberta iela in Rīga is a bit like visiting an abandoned film studio where a biblical epic, a gothic gore-fest and a children's fairy tale were being filmed at the same time. Imperious stone sphinxes stand guard outside no. 2, while malevolent gape-mouthed satyrs gaze down from the facade across the street. Further down at no. 11, a grey apartment block with steep-pitched roofs and asymmetrical windows looks like an oversized farmhouse squatted by a community of Transylvanian counts.

Alberta iela is the most spectacular street in a city that is famous for its eccentric buildings – products of a pre-World War I construction boom that saw architects indulge in all manner of decorative obsessions. Many of the structures dating from this period are described in the guidebooks as Art Nouveau, although the sheer range of eye-catching embellishments suggests a much wider palette of influences.

Most influential of the local architects was Mikhail Eisenstein, father of Soviet film director Sergei. Responsible for the sphinx-house at Alberta iela 2, Eisenstein filled his designs with Egyptian, Greek and Roman-inspired details, producing buildings that looked like extravagantly iced cakes adorning the party-table of a deranged emperor. The most famous of his creations is just around the corner from Alberta iela at Elizabetes 10, a purple-and-cream confection with a scarily huge pair of female heads staring impassively from the pediment.

An imprint of equal substance was left on the city by Latvian architect Eižens Laube, who brought the folk architecture of the Baltic country cottage into the heart of the city. The apartment block at Alberta iela 11 is very much his trademark, employing shingled roofs and soaring pointy gables to produce a disconcerting half-breed borne of gingerbread house and Gotham City. Something of an architectural equivalent to the Brothers Grimm, Laube's creations add a compellingly moody character to the bustling boulevards of Rīga's main shopping and business districts.

Rīga's Art Nouveau-period apartment blocks seem all the more incongruous when you consider that they were built to house the stolid middle-class citizens of a down-to-earth mercantile city. Judging by the sheer number of stuccoed sprites, mythical animals and come-hither mermaids staring out from the city's facades, psychoanalysts would have had a field day analyzing the architectural tastes of Rīga's pre-World War I bourgeoisie.

need to know
Alberta iela lies in the Centrs district of Rīga. For more information see Ⓦ www. rigatourism.com.

Try imagining Pompeii still existing as a functioning twenty-first-century city, and you'll probably get a good idea of what the Croatian port of Split looks like. At its heart lies a confusing warren of narrow streets, crooked alleys and Corinthian-style colonnades that looks like a computer-generated reconstruction of an archeological dig. High-street shops, banks, restaurants and bars seem stuffed into this structure like incongruous afterthoughts.

Split began life as the purpose-built palace of Roman Emperor Diocletian, who retired here after his abdication in 305 AD. When marauding Avars sacked the nearby city of Salona in 615, fleeing inhabitants sought refuge within the palace walls, improvising a home in what must have been the most grandiose squat of all time. Diocletian's mausoleum was turned into a cathedral, the Temple of Jupiter became a baptistery, and medieval tenement blocks were built into the palace walls.

Nowadays the palace's crumbling courtyards provide the perfect setting for some of the best bars in the Mediterranean. The only problem is that Split's maze-like street plan makes it head-scratchingly difficult to navigate your way back to the welcoming drinking hole you discovered the previous night. Split folk themselves possess a highly developed system of nocturnal radar, flitting from one place to the next without ever staying anywhere long enough to make it look as if they haven't got a better party to go to.

The best way not to get disoriented is to locate Dosud, a split-level zigzag of an alley in the southwestern corner of the palace. Here you'll find ultra-trendy Puls, whose post-industrial interior and cushion-splashed stone-stepped terrace is an essential stop on any bar crawl; and its polar opposite, Tri Volta, a resolutely old-fashioned local that has long catered to neighbourhood bohemians. In between the two is Ghetto, a temple to graffiti art with a beautiful flower-filled courtyard which occasionally hosts al fresco gigs. History doesn't record whether Diocletian was much of a drinker, but this proudly pagan emperor would have approved of Split's enduring appetite for Bacchic indulgence.

need to know

Tri Volta, Ghetto and Puls are officially only open until midnight, but tend to keep on serving as long as they feel they can get away with it.

22
Vulture-watching in the Madzharovo **Nature Reserve**, Bulgaria

You are crouched in juniper bushes exuding the smell of gin when suddenly the wind shifts and a foul odour sweeps through the gorge. From their perch halfway up the cliffs, three vultures launch themselves onto the thermals before plunging into the thickets of Salix trees, emerging with their talons and beaks laden with rotting flesh. Refocusing your binoculars, you track them back to their nests, where they start to feed a ravenous brood of chicks.

Vulture-watching at Bulgaria's *Madzharovo* nature reserve isn't your standard ornithological experience. Vultures are ugly, vicious creatures that feed on carrion; their intestinal systems have evolved to handle any microbe nature can throw at them. The Arda gorge is one of the few breeding grounds in Europe for Egyptian, Griffon and black vultures; here twitchers can also spot eight kinds of falcons and nine kinds of woodpecker as well as black storks, bee-eaters, olive-tree warblers, and several species of bats.

All this wildlife is right on the doorstep of an ex-mining town of crumbling concrete low-rises – a juxtaposition of magnificent nature and man-made stagnation that's all too common in the Rhodope Mountains.

With its forests of pine and spruce, alpine meadows, crags and gorges, this is one of the wildest and most beautiful regions of Bulgaria. Travelling to the reserve through its villages, you're struck by the degrees of separation between its Christian and Pomak (Slav Muslim) inhabitants, with some villages exclusively one, others a mixture of both – signified by churches and mosques, miniskirts and veils. With villages half-depopulated by the flight of able-bodied adults to richer nations of the European Union, and remaining subsistence farmers too poor to afford pesticides or herbicides, the land is as ecologically rich as it is economically blighted.

need to know

From Bulgaria's second city, Plovdiv, take a bus from the Yug terminal to the town of Haskovo (1hr 30min) in time to catch the 3pm bus to *Madzharovo* (2hr). The Nature Information Centre (Mon–Fri 9am-5pm; ℡03720/345, ✉ marin.kurtev@bspb.org), arranges guided tours of the reserve.

23

Crossing cultural boundaries in **Kraków**

is May 2005 and Poland's oldest football team, Cracovia Kraków, are playing a crucial end-of-season fixture against second-division promotion rivals Pogon Szczecin. Cracovia's stadium, an old-fashioned arena of banked-earthed terraces, is besieged by what seems to be the biggest horde of skinheads ever assembled in one place. The only adult male present **with any hair**, I pass gingerly through the turnstiles and try to blend in by joining the queue at the sausage stand. In the event the crowd is as good tempered as they come: Cracovia secure the point they need, and the orc-like army depart in a happy mood.

Cracovia's supporters weren't always such a **uniform bunch**. In fact the club serves as a metaphor for the multicultural history of the city. During the interwar years, Cracovia were nicknamed the "Yids" because significant members of Kraków's Jewish community could be found on both the terraces and the team sheet. They also happened to be the favourite team of local boy Karol Wojtyła, the future **Pope John Paul II**.

Before World War II, many of Cracovia's supporters came from Kazimierz, the inner-city suburb where Poles and Jews had lived cheek-by-jowl for centuries. Most of Kazimierz's Jews perished in the nearby camps of **Płaszów and Auschwitz**, but their synagogues and tenement houses remain, providing a walk-round history lesson in Jewish heritage and culture. Kazimierz's complex identity is underlined by the presence of some of Kraków's most revered medieval churches. The weekend after the Cracovia match, I watch the suburb's narrow streets swell with the solemn, banner-bearing **Corpus Christi processions** that are among the best-attended events in the Polish Catholic calendar.

Today Kazimierz's Jewish population is a **tiny fraction** of what it was in the 1930s, but the district retains a vibrant melting-pot atmosphere – thanks in large part to its varied population of working-class Poles, impoverished artists, and inner-city-lifestyle-addicted yuppies. The most dramatic change of recent years has been its reinvention as a bohemian nightlife district, full of zanily decorated cellar bars, pubs that look like antique shops, and **cafés that double as art galleries**. With the area's non-conformist, anything-goes atmosphere drawing increasing numbers of the open-minded, tolerant and curious, Kazimierz is emerging once more as a unique incubator of cultural exchange.

need to know

The tourist information office is at ul. Jozefa 7 (Mon–Fri 10am–4pm; ⓦ www.krakow.
pl). The Cracovia stadium lies west of the town centre on al. Focha

24 BUNKERING DOWN in Durres, Albania

A small rickety Ferris wheel now turns on the spot in Skanderbeg Square where Enver Hoxha's colossal gilded statue once stood. After his death in 1985, Hoxha's busts were gradually removed from public view and the National Historical Museum in Tirana was "ideologically renovated". However, despite the cosmetic surgery, Albania just can't seem to shrug off one legacy of Hoxha's brutal brand of Stalinism.

The ultra-paranoid dictator covered Albania's pretty rural landscape with over 700,000 bunkers – one for every four citizens – to protect his people from invading hordes of imperialists, fascists and counter-revolutionaries. The enemy tanks never arrived, but the bunkers were built so strongly that to this day few have been removed. These small concrete domes occupy every possible vantage point in the rolling countryside that flanks the road between the capital and the port city of Durres on the Adriatic coast: gloomy relics of the old regime that have been reinvented to represent the spirit of the new Albania.

The rusty ledge of one bunker's entrance is lined with pretty potted flowers, while rows of tomatoes grow defiantly around it. Inside, candles struggle to stay alight in the stale air, scarcely lighting the table around which a family of five, who have chosen to call this suffocating box home, are eating dinner. Other bunkers are painted with jaunty murals or emblazoned with the colours of football teams or lovers' names: unambiguous expressions of the new priorities in Albanians' lives. A young couple emerges from a solitary bunker on the brow of a hill, walks down to a beaten-up Mercedes parked by the roadside and stops for a lingering kiss before driving back to Tirana.

And at Durres, the odd imperialist tourist freshly arrived on the ferry from Italy sips beer and listens to one ABBA hit after another in the dark, slightly dank surroundings of a beachside bunker bar, as Hoxha turns lividly in his grave.

need to know
Several European airlines fly to Tirana; there is also a ferry service from Bari, Italy to Durres. Buses run regularly from Tirana to Durres and take about 1 hour.

It's not often you're invited to join a guided tour of a nuclear missile base, especially when you're in the middle of one of northeastern Europe's most idyllic areas of unspoiled wilderness. However, this is exactly what's on offer at the friendly tourist information centre at Plateliai, the rustic, timber-built village in the centre of western Lithuania's *Zemaitija National Park*.

Long popular with a happy-go-lucky bunch of Lithuanian hostellers, campers and canoeists, the park is famous for its emblematic Baltic landscape. Calm grey lakes are fringed by squelchy bogs, forests of silver birch, and intricately carved wooden crosses which sprout from farmhouse gardens like totem poles. It's perversely appropriate that Soviet military planners chose this tranquil spot as the perfect place to hide a rocket base. Located at the end of a harmless-looking gravel track, the Plokštinė base is virtually invisible at ground level, its low-lying grey-green domes blending sympathetically with the local landscape of stubby coniferous shrubs. There's no front door: an innocuous-looking metal panel opens to reveal a staircase, descending into an abandoned world of concrete-floored, metal-doored rooms, linked by passageways which bring to mind the galleries of an underground cave system.

Built in 1962, the installation at Plokštinė was one of the first such sites in the then Soviet Union, housing four nuclear missiles capable of hitting targets throughout Western and southern Europe. Closed down in 1978 and left to rot, it's now eerily empty of any signs, panels or technical equipment that would indicate its previous purpose.

Until that is, you come to one of the silos themselves – a vast, metal-lined cylindrical pit deep enough to accommodate 22 metres of slender, warhead-tipped rocket. The missile itself was evacuated long ago, but peering into the abyss from the maintenance gallery can still be a heart-stopping experience. Especially when you consider that similar silos, from North America to North Korea, are still very much in working order.

need to know

Tours of the Plokštinė missile base are organized by the National Park Information Centre in Plateliai (ⓦ www.zemaitijosnp.lt). Hostel-style accommodation can be arranged from €10 per person.

25 Ultimate

experiences

Eastern Europe

miscellany

1 ▌ Where is Eastern Europe?

As an entity, Eastern Europe is generally thought to comprise the countries behind what used to be known as the "Iron Curtain": as they now stand, these are Poland, the Czech and Slovak Republics, Hungary, Slovenia, Croatia, Bosnia and Herzegovina, Serbia, Montenegro, Macedonia, Albania, Romania, Bulgaria, Estonia, Latvia, Lithuania, Belarus, Ukraine, Moldova and part of Russia.

"From Stettin in the Baltic to Trieste in the Adriatic, an iron curtain has descended across the continent."
Winston Churchill in March 1946, on the extent of postwar Soviet control over Eastern Europe.

2 ▌ Meat and two veg

Eastern European food is generally heavy on animal flesh, beetroot and cabbage. Vegetarians take note: ham and salami are not considered to be meat in this part of the world and come under veggie sections on the menu. The northern nations take their culinary influences from Germany and Scandinavia, whereas southern countries take their cues from Greece, Turkey and Georgia. Some national dishes to consider are:

"Ukrainian Snickers" raw pig fat with rye bread
Fried potatoes and onions a dish so hallowed in Slovenia that it has its own festival
Kukurec Albanian speciality of stuffed sheep's intestines
Verivorst and mulgikkapsad Estonian blood sausage with sauerkraut
Kavarma stew of pork, tomatoes, lard and leeks, beloved in Bulgaria

3 Cool as a cucumber

If a Czech thinks he's been asked an obvious question he may reply "I'm not here for the blueberries", whereas if involved in a boring activity may claim, "it's like throwing peas at a wall". A Bulgarian might warn you not to carry two melons under the same armpit. If a Russian tells you you look like a cucumber, say thank you, but be upset if you are called an old horseradish; a pointless activity may be compared to "knocking pears out of a tree with your dick".

"Don't walk around hot porridge!"

Czech saying

3 Top tipples

Calling someone a teetotaller in Eastern Europe usually just means that they don't drink spirits – every day. As well as the usual selection, each country has its own particular liquor, made with local fruit or herbs; if you are (un)lucky you may get to down a homemade version.

▶▶ **The best drinks to try**

Vodka drunk throughout the region, it's warming and supposedly aids digestion.

Beer Poles and Balts make lovely malty dark versions, but Czechs, since they invented it, have the best lager.

Brandy Moldovans modestly claim theirs is the finest in Europe.

Champagne Crimean, though no rival to French, is perfectly palatable – and far cheaper.

Wine Bulgarian, Hungarian and Romanian vintages are very decent; best of all is Tokaj, the world-renowned Hungarian dessert wine.

Borovička a gorgeous Slovak sloe spirit, similar to, yet more fiery than gin.

Sljivovica Serbian liquor made from plums, popular throughout the Balkans.

Raki the staple Albanian tipple, distilled by home brewers across the land.

"A good wine doesn't need a label."

Hungarian saying

5 Balaclava-wearing vampires

The vampire (Serbian) in a balaclava (Ukrainian) sat in a coach (Hungarian), using a biro (Hungarian) to tot up his bridge (Russian) score while the sleazy (Latvian) Cossack (Ukrainian) waved his sabre (Hungarian) at the cravat (Croatian)-wearing cosmonaut (Russian); the robot (Czech) shot a horde (Polish) of mammoths (Russian) with a pistol (Czech). They all retired to a bistro (Russian) to talk (Lithuanian) and eat some pastrami (Romanian).

6 East European émigrés

Waves of immigration brought about by poverty, anti-Semitism, war, defections, and the opening up of the eastern bloc brought some of the greatest icons of the twentieth century from Eastern Europe to the west. The following is just a selection of people born in the countries given (as they now stand):

Belarus artist Marc Chagall; MGM founder Louis B Mayer; sci-fi author Isaac Asimov.

Bulgaria conceptual "wrapping" artist Christo.

Czech Republic playwright Tom Stoppard; Wonderbra model Eva Herzigova; former US Secretary of State Madeleine Albright.

Hungary actor Béla Lugosi; escapologist Harry Houdini; founder of Fox Studios William Fox.

Latvia artist Mark Rothko; political philosopher Isaiah Berlin.

Lithuania sculptor Jacques Lipschitz.

Macedonia Mother Teresa.

Poland MGM chief Sam Goldwyn; make-up empire founder Helena Rubinstein; composer and pianist Frédéric Chopin; Pope John Paul II.

Romania actor Edward G. Robinson; Pop Idol wannabes the Cheeky Girls.

Russia *White Christmas* composer Irving Berlin.

Slovakia actor Peter Lorre; media mogul Robert Maxwell.

Ukraine author Joseph Conrad; model-turned-actress Milla Jovovich.

7 Top ten discoveries and inventions

Ball-point pens László Bíró (Hungary)
Semtex Stanislav Brebera and Bohumil Šole (Czech Republic)
Lager developed at the Plzen brewery (Czech Republic)
The helicopter Igor Sikorsky (Ukraine)
The periodic table Dimitri Mendeleyev (Russia)
Yoghurt Bulgars left their milk to ferment in goatskin bags
Modern astronomy (and the discovery that the earth orbits the sun) Copernicus (Poland)
Radium Marie Curie (Poland)
Alternating electric currents Nikola Tesla (Serbia)
The parachute Štefan Banič (Slovakia)

"A man goes into his local garage and asks, 'Do you have a windscreen wiper for my Škoda?' 'Sounds like a fair swap', replied the man in the garage."

One of many jokes about the Czech car, whose name unfortunately means "pity" or "shame" in Czech

8 Revolutions

Match the revolutions with the countries:

A Orange	1 Poland
B Velvet	2 Estonia
C Singing	3 Czechoslovakia
D Solidarity	4 Ukraine

(answers: A/4, B/3, C/2, D/1).

9 Eastern Europe on Film

Before the Rain (1994). Told in three parts, this beautifully shot Macedonian film is an uncompromising love story set against the backdrop of the Balkan wars.

Burnt by the Sun (1994). Oscar-winning Chekhovian tale of betrayal set in prewar Stalinist Russia. Nikita Mikhalkov masterfully writes, directs and stars.

Kolya (1996). Cross-cultural comedy set in pre-Velvet Revolution Prague about a Czech musician forced to look after a Russian boy – it won an Oscar.

No Man's Land (2001). Deeply affecting and darkly comic Oscar-winning movie about a Bosnian and a Serb trapped together in a trench.

The Pianist (2002). Roman Polanski's elegant film about a Polish Jewish musician's survival in the Warsaw ghetto during World War II.

Time of the Gypsies (1989). Ethereal, compassionate and witty film about this most marginalized of races by Bosnian director Emir Kusturica, featuring a sublime soundtrack. See also the same director's *Underground* (1995).

10 From Paris to Prague

Looking for somewhere that resembles nineteenth-century Paris or London, Nottingham in the Middle Ages or Civil war-era Carolina? Since the fall of communism, the picturesque cities and countryside of Eastern Europe – and its cheap crews – have proved a magnet for location scouts for TV and film.

• The queen of the shoots is Prague, which has stood in for Victorian London in (among others) *From Hell* (with Johnny Depp as Jack the Ripper) and Roman Polanski's *Oliver Twist*, as well as Hamburg (*Swing Kids*), Vienna (*The Illusionist*), New Jersey (*Hellboy*), Zurich (*The Bourne Identity*), Paris (*Les Miserables*), and Miami (*Casino Royale*).

• A Soviet sports' stadium in Vilnius stands in for Whitehall palace in *Elizabeth I*.

• Transylvania becomes 1860s North Carolina in *Cold Mountain*.

• Fot, near Budapest, housed Robin Hood and his merry men for the 2006 BBC series.

- Ukrainian birch trees pose as Chinese bamboo in *The House of Flying Daggers*.
- 1930s Los Angeles is transported to Bulgaria in *The Black Dahlia*.

11 When in...

▶▶ Ten must reads

Transylvania, Romania Bram Stoker's *Dracula*

Moscow, Russia Mikhail Bulgakov's *Master and Marguerite*

St Petersburg, Russia Fyodor Dostoevsky's *Crime and Punishment*

Prague, Czech Republic Bohumil Hrabal's *I served the King of England*

Sofia, Bulgaria Georgi Gospodinov's *Natural Novel*

Odessa, Ukraine Isaac Babel's *Odessa Tales*

Gdansk, Poland Günter Grass's *The Tin Drum*

Kaunas, Lithuania Czesław Miłosz's *The Issa Valley*

Vilnius, Lithuania Stephan Collishaw's *The Last Girl*

Bosnia-Hercegovina Ivo Andrič's *Bridge over the Drina*

12 Dastardly dictators

Eastern Europe in the twentieth century has hardly been short of its dictators – witness the following:

Joseph Stalin ("Uncle Joe", 1878–1953), granddaddy of them all and creator of the original totalitarian state in the Soviet Union.

Enver Hoxha ("The Ugly One", 1908–85), an avowed Stalinist who managed to isolate Albania from the rest of Europe during his forty-year rule.

Nicolae Ceaușescu ("The Conducator", 1918–89), megalomaniac Romanian who was deposed and executed in December 1989 during the most dramatic and bloodiest of all the communist revolutions.

Slobodan Milošević ("The Butcher of the Balkans", 1941–2006), arch-architect of the break-up of Yugoslavia, who then oversaw the ruination of Serbia before being carted off to The Hague where he subsequently died.

Aleksandr Lukashenko ("Papa", 1954–), president of Belarus since 1994, having abolished the constitutional limit to presidential terms. A self-confessed "authoritarian" ruler, he still uses the KGB to silence dissenters. Known as "Europe's last dictator".

13 Music to the ears

▸▸ Five Eastern European sounds

Boban Markovič Orchestra The Serbian trumpet maestro and his marvellous twelve-piece orchestra are the undisputed kings of Balkan brass.

Gogol Bordello Consisting mainly of East European immigrants led by the charismatic Ukrainian Eugene Hutz, this New York-based gypsy punk outfit have become firm favourites thanks to their manic live shows.

Laibach Legendary alternative Slovenian rock group who came to the fore in the early 1980s with their trademark militant/industrial sound. They're still recording and touring.

Na na The Russian Take That, who specialized in getting girls to come on stage and strip them of their rustic/partisan outfits to reveal synthetic black string vests and pants. Definitely ripe for a comeback.

Taraf de Haidouks Outstanding Romanian gypsy ensemble who combine outrageous talent and ebullient musicianship to dazzling effect.

14 Did you know...?

The geographical centre of Europe is located 25km north of Vilnius.

15 Sporting stars

Eastern European nations have a fantastically rich sporting heritage, and the following individuals have attained sporting immortality:

Hungarian fencer **Aladár Gerevich** who racked up an incredible six Olympic titles between 1932 and 1960.

Czech long-distance runner **Emil Zátopek** who won three gold medals at the 1952 Olympic games, in the 5000m, 10000m and marathon races.

Romanian gymnast **Nadia Comaneci** who, at the 1976 Montreal Olympics, aged just 14, won three gold medals and became the first gymnast in Olympic history to achieve a perfect 10 score.

▸▸ Fantasy football all-time East European 11

The region has given us some pretty decent footballers, too:

1 **Lev Yashin** (USSR)
2 **József Bozsik** (Hungary)
3 **Nándor Hidegkuti** (Hungary)
4 **Nemanja Vidić** (Serbia)
5 **Josef Masopust** (Czechoslovakia)
6 **Pavel Nedvéd** (Czech Republic)
7 **Andriy Shevchenko** (Ukraine)
8 **Hristo Stoichkov** (Bulgaria)
9 **Ferenc Puskás** (Hungary)
10 **Gheorghe Hagi** (Romania)
11 **Oleg Blokhin** (USSR)

16 Five East European festivals

Ski-flying World Championships Kranjska Gora, Slovenia (March). Beer, music and much merriment – oh, and some ski-jumping too.
Pageant of the Juni Brașov, Romania (April). Spectacular procession of costumed *juni* (young men), with brass bands in tow.
St John's Day Warsaw, Kraków and Poznań (June 23/24). Poland's major rivers come alight with candles and fireworks and boat parades.
Exit Novi Sad, Serbia (July). Eastern Europe's most up-for-it rock festival, featuring some of the world's finest bands performing in the grounds of Petrovaradin Fortress by the Danube.
Song Festivals Baltic States. Each state holds a massive folk song festival every 4–5 years.

17 Eurovision Song Contest

Although Yugoslavia won the Eurovision Song Contest in 1989, no current Eastern European nation had managed to capture this most dubious of titles until Estonia emerged victorious in 2001. This kick-started an impressive run of success, with Latvia, in 2002, and the Ukraine, in 2004, both coming first. Two of the contest's more controversial acts in recent times were the Russian female duo **T.a.T.u**, who caused a bit of a storm thanks to marketing themselves as a (faux) lesbian couple, and **Sestre** ("Sisters"), three Slovenian transvestites who performed as air-hostesses.

"We are the winners of Eurovision

We are, we are! We are, we are!

We are the winners of Eurovision

We are, we are! We are, we are!"

Lithuanian entry 2006 by LT United. Lithuania remains the only Baltic state yet to win the Eurovision Song Contest.

18 The Gypsies

One of the world's greatest concentration of **Gypsies** – or Roma to give them their correct ethnic title – are to be found in Eastern Europe, and in particular the Balkan peninsula. From the moment they arrived in the region – many suppose from India, via Egypt (hence the name "gypsy") – around the fourteenth century, the Roma were subject to persecution and prejudice, and nowhere more so than in the forced labour camps of World War II, where at least half a million were killed in a genocide known as the *Porajmos*. In communist times Roma experienced assimilation schemes and widespread cultural exclusion, practices that continue today in some states.

19 Ten largest Eastern European cities

Moscow (pop. 10.5m)
St Petersburg (pop. 4.7m)
Kiev (pop. 2.7m)
Bucharest (pop. 2m)
Minsk (pop. 1.8m)
Budapest (pop. 1.7m)
Warsaw (pop. 1.7m)
Belgrade (pop. 1.6m)
Sofia (pop. 1.3m)
Prague (pop. 1.2m)

20 East European Jews

Before World War II, Eastern Europe had the largest Jewish population in the world. Historically, Jews had suffered exclusion from many parts of Europe, but since 1791 had been allowed to live in the Pale of Settlement – an area established by Catherine the Great, which covered much of Eastern Poland and Russia. In the twentieth century, this is where the majority of Europe's Jews still remained, many of them in *shtetls* – predominantly Jewish small towns, where they had been forced to live having been previously excluded from cities. With the Nazi takeover of Eastern Europe, aided by strong feelings of local anti-Semitism, all but a remnant of the Jewish population was murdered. Of the fraction who remained, many fought as partisans, or were able to hide undiscovered. Since the demise of communism there has been a rekindling of interest in Jewish life such as new cultural centres, renovated synagogues and theatres in many of the places where their loss was felt so strongly, in particular in the cities of Vilnius and Kraków.

21 Ten outstanding natural attractions

Škocjan Caves, Slovenia Magnificent underground canyon in the heart of the Slovenian Karst.

Plitvice Lakes, Croatia A mesmerising chain of forest-fringed lakes, waterfalls and rapids.

Carpathian Mountains, Romania/Ukraine Stunning hiking terrain sheltering quaint villages and home to some fabulous wildlife, including wolves and brown bears.

Lake Ohrid, Macedonia Straddling Macedonia and Albania, this is one of the world's deepest and clearest lakes.

High Tatras, Slovakia Jagged, granite peaks rising spectacularly from the Poprad Plain.

Couronian Spit, Lithuania Dramatic landscape of pine forests, pristine sands and calm lagoons.

Tara Canyon, Montenegro Wild and wonderful, this is Europe's deepest canyon.

The Danube River From the Black Forest to the Black Sea, this majestic waterway is Europe's second longest (2857km) after the Volga in Russia.

Lake Héviz, Hungary The largest thermal lake in the world.

Puszcza Białowieska, Poland A national park containing the last major tract of primeval forest left in Europe.

22 Etiquette

Bulgarians shake their heads when they mean "yes" and nod when they mean "no".

In a Czech pub never top up a new glass of beer with the remains of the previous one.

When a Russian lights a cigarette, wish him good health, however ironic it seems.

23 Old Mr Chlapitsky had a farm

Many **East European expressions** seem to revolve around the farmyard:

I'll slap you so hard you'll see green horses (a **Romanian** threat).

You're as fat as a sheep's knees (**Romanian** for slim).

You're like a cow with a new gate in front of her (**Romanian** for "you look lost").

I'll do it when it's the horse's Easter (**Romanian** for "never").

A steel mare goes barefoot (**Czech** saying).

You ox! (A **Czech** insult – though friendly too, like "mate").

You can't get bacon from a dog (**Hungarian** for "a leopard can't change its spots").

A hungry pig always thinks about acorns ("you can't teach an old dog new tricks" in **Hungarian**).

The owl shouldn't tell the sparrow he has a big head (**Hungarian** for the pot calling the kettle black).

Don't go into the forest if you don't like wolves (**Russian** saying).

God's cow, fly away to heaven, where your children are eating cutlets (**Russian** equivalent to "Ladybird, ladybird, fly away home").

"It is better to have ten friends than one enemy."

Polish saying

24 Fluctuating boundaries

The **territories and borders** of Eastern Europe have changed constantly throughout the centuries. Many of the countries were created or made independent in treaties following World War I; Montenegro is the most recent to gain independence (2006). Depending on who was in power, some places have suffered almost continuous name changes – for example, in the last century L'viv (now in west Ukraine), was known as Lwow (Polish), Lemburg (German) and Lvov (Russian) before becoming L'viv again.

25 Five interesting places to stay

Do time in Vaclav Havel's cell at the Unitas Hotel, Prague, a former prison.

Feel like you're in a John le Carré novel at the Palace Athena Hotel, Bucharest – a hive of espionage activity during the Cold War.

Bed down in a monk's bunk in the stunning but spartan Rila monastery, Bulgaria.

Sleep in the communist police force's former HQ in Budapest – now, snubbingly, transformed into the luxury Le Meridien hotel.

Spend a night in the Celica, Llubljana's hippest hostel – a barracks in a former life, each room is given a different theme by a local artist.

Ultimate experiences

Eastern Europe

small print

ROUGH GUIDES – don't just travel

We hope you've been inspired by the experiences in this book. To us, they sum up what makes Eastern Europe such an extraordinary and stimulating region to travel. There are 24 other books in the 25 Ultimate Experiences series, each conceived to whet your appetite for travel and for everything the world has to offer. As well as covering the globe, the 25s series also includes books on **Journeys, World Food, Adventure Travel, Places to Stay, Ethical Travel, Wildlife Adventures** and **Wonders of the World**.

When you start planning your trip, Rough Guides' new-look guides, maps and phrasebooks are the ultimate companions. For 25 years we've been refining what makes a good guidebook and we now include more colour photos and more information – on average 50% more pages – than any of our competitors. Just look for the sky-blue spines.

Rough Guides don't just travel – we also believe in getting the most out of life without a passport. Since the publication of the bestselling Rough Guides to **The Internet** and **World Music**, we've brought out a wide range of lively and authoritative guides on everything from **Climate Change** to **Hip-Hop**, from **MySpace** to **Film Noir** and from **The Brain** to **The Rolling Stones**.

Publishing information

Rough Guide 25 Ultimate experiences Eastern Europe Published May 2007 by Rough Guides Ltd, 80 Strand, London WC2R 0RL
345 Hudson St, 4th Floor, New York, NY 10014, USA
14 Local Shopping Centre, Panchsheel Park, New Delhi 110017, India
Distributed by the Penguin Group
Penguin Books Ltd,
80 Strand, London WC2R 0RL
Penguin Group (USA)
375 Hudson Street, NY 10014, USA
Penguin Group (Australia)
250 Camberwell Road, Camberwell, Victoria 3124, Australia
Penguin Books Canada Ltd,
10 Alcorn Avenue, Toronto, Ontario, Canada M4V 1E4
Penguin Group (NZ)
67 Apollo Drive, Mairangi Bay, Auckland 1310, New Zealand
Printed in China

80pp
A catalogue record for this book is available from the British Library
ISBN: 978-1-84353-818-9

The publishers and authors have done their best to ensure the accuracy and currency of all the information in Rough Guide 25 Ultimate experiences Eastern Europe, however, they can accept no responsibility for any loss, injury, or inconvenience sustained by any traveller as a result of information or advice contained in the guide.

1   3   5   7   9   8   6   4   2

Rough Guide credits

Editor: Alison Murchie
Design & picture research: Dan May, Chloë Faram
Cartography: Katie Lloyd-Jones, Maxine Repath
Cover design: Diana Jarvis, Chloë Roberts
Production: Aimee Hampson, Katherine Owers
Proofreader: Edward Aves

The authors

Jon Bousfield (experiences 1, 4, 10, 14, 20, 21, 23, 25) is the author of Rough Guides to the Baltic States and Croatia, and co-author of Rough Guides to Bulgaria and Poland.

Rob Humphreys (experiences 2, 12, 17) is the author of Rough Guides to the Czech and Slovak Republics and Prague.

Lily Hyde (experience 3) has worked and travelled extensively as a journalist in Eastern Europe.

Norm Longley (experiences 5, 6, 7, 9, 13, 15, 18, 19 and miscellany) is the author of the Rough Guide to Slovenia, and co-author of Rough Guides to Hungary and Romania.

Dan Richardson (experiences 8, 16, 22) is the author of Rough Guides to Moscow and St Petersburg, and co-author of Rough Guides to Budapest, Bulgaria and Hungary.

Alison Murchie (experience 11 and miscellany) is a travel editor at Rough Guides and previously lived and worked in Eastern Europe.

Ross Velton (experience 24) lived and worked in Albania.

Picture credits

Cover Baths in Budapest © Ami Vitale/Alamy
2 Łódź building © Mark Pink/Alamy
6 *Worker and Farm Girl* statue © Terence Waelan/Alamy
8-9 Tkalcica street, Zagreb © Globe exposure/Alamy
10-11 *Bieres de la Meuse* by Alphons Mucha © Christie's images/Corbis; woman drinking beer © Edward Longmire/Alamy
13 Hammer and sickle © Emmanuel Faure/Getty; *Worker and Farm Girl* statue © Terence Waelan/Alamy
14-15 Lahemaa National Park © allOver Photography/Alamy; European beaver © Niall Benvie/Corbis
16-17 *MS Dammacia* cruise ship in Kotor bay © SIME/Thiele Klaus/4cornersimages.com
18-19 Budapest baths © Mark Thomas
21 Fresco of Vlad the Impaler © Clive Tully/Alamy; Bran castle © Catherine Karnow/Corbis
22-23 St Petersburg ravers © Jeremy Nicholl/Alamy; sunrise on the palace embankment © Dean Conger/Corbis
24-25 Music fan at Guča festival © Dragan Karadarevic/Reuters/Corbis
26-27 Łódź building © Mark Pink/Alamy; Manufaktura, Łódź © Philippe Giraud
28-29 Decorative teapot © Vilnius, Keren S/Corbis; Vilnius street © Pascal Le Segretain/Corbis
30-31 Dobroslava church, Slovakia © isifa Image Service s.r.o/Alamy; wooden planks © David Lyons/Alamy
32-33 Barman pouring shot © Sue Cunningham photographs; Belgrade nightlife © Jason Manning/PYMCA
34-35 Goats and sleeping herdsman © blickwinkel/Alamy

36-37 Postojna caves © Ladislav Janicek/zefa/Corbis; Proteus Anguinus © Ladi Kirn/Alamy
38-39 Visitor reflected in Rembrandt's *Portrait of an Old Man* © Alexander Demianchuk/Reuters/Corbis; Murillo's *The Immaculate Conception* © Archivo Iconografico, S.A.
40-41 Detail of tomb of St John of Nepomuk © AA World Travel Library/Alamy
42-43 Valley of the Lakes, Triglav © Robert Preston/Alamy
44-45 Wine cellar, Tokaj region © isifa Image Service s.r.o/Alamy; harvesting grapes in Kiraly Hegy vineyard © Herbert Lehmann/Cephas Picture Library/Alamy; grapes close-ups – green and red © Ian O'Leary/RG/DK
46-47 Art Nouveau figures © Demetrio Carrasco/RG/DK; 10b Elisabetes Street © Demetrio Carrasco/RG/DK; Art Nouveau face detail © David Borland/RG/DK; reflections © David Borland/RG/DK; Art Nouveau Façade © David Borland/RG/DK; Art Nouveau detail © David Borland/RG/DK
48-49 Diocletian's palace © Split, Lucio Rossi/DK
50-51 Vultures in the Madzharovo reserve © blickwinkel/Alamy; gorge near Kurdalj © Vladimir Alexeev/Alamy
52-53 *Alchemia* bar, Krakow © croftsphoto/Alamy; Star of David in the Tempel Synagogue, Kazimierz © Colin Pantall/Alamy
54-55 Shengjin beach © Roland Liptak/Alamy; snapshots of Albania © Richard Wayman/Corbis Sygma; painted bunker © Michel Setboun/Corbis
56-57 Plokštiné missile base photos © Andrius Vanagas
58 Murillo's *The Immaculate Conception* © Archivo Iconografico, S.A.

Fly Less – Stay Longer!

Rough Guides believes in the good that travel does, but we are deeply aware of the impact of fuel emissions on climate change. We recommend taking fewer trips and staying for longer. If you can avoid travelling by air, please use an alternative, especially for journeys of under 1000km/600miles. And always offset your travel at www.roughguides.com/climatechange.

ROUGH
DES

ROUGH
GUIDES

ROUGH
GUIDES

ROUGH
GUIDES

ROUGH
GUIDES

ROUGH
GUIDES

New Zealand

Budapest

Thailand

Greece

Punk

Italy

India

Over 70 reference books and hundreds of travel
guides, maps & phrasebooks that cover the world